Messages from
The Three Sisters
Volume 3

Gregory A. Kompes

FABULIST FLASH PUBLISHING, LTD.
LAS VEGAS, NEVADA

Messages from The Three Sisters, Volume 3
Copyright © 2015 by Gregory A. Kompes

Published by Fabulist Flash Publishing, Ltd.

Print Edition

ISBN: 978-0-9793612-6-5

Exterior Cover Photo
© 2013 by Gregory A. Kompes

Fabulist Flash Publishing, Ltd.
PO Box 570368
Las Vegas, NV 89157

Dedicated
to my friends at
The Universal Wisdom Center.

Table of Contents

Contents

Contents

Contents

Contents

Contents

Contents

Contents

Contents

Contents

Messages from
The Three Sisters
Volume 3

We, The Three Sisters...

We, The Three Sisters, have decided that now is the time to communicate our thoughts and messages with you because we have entered a new phase of enlightenment. The young ones coming forth don't need our guidance, for they are connected in a stronger way to their own source energy understanding. It is those of you who have been in physical for some time that will benefit most from that which we have to share.

This new phase of enlightenment will continue whether you participate or not. We do believe though that you will benefit greatly, you will find this phase of human experience more fun, more joyful, and more regarding, if you allow yourself to open more to the experience, if you allow yourself to experience this experience.

It may be difficult if you only approach the time of enlightenment through your lens of past experience. There are negative connotations about spirituality, new age, and the like. What we ask of you is to not look backward, but instead look forward. Where is it that you would like to be? How is it that you would like to feel? If it is a better feeling you seek, feelings of love, joy, and happiness, then we offer that you would benefit from not looking backward at your past experiences and past emotions, and instead, look forward to how you would like to feel. Just that simple idea will raise your vibration. Just looking forward and wanting to feel happier, joyful, and filled with love will help you move toward those wonderful feelings.

Today is a new beginning

*T*oday is a new beginning. Nothing is set in stone or archived. Each moment is it's on experience. The now that you are living in is fleeting and changeable. So, let go of the past. Begin fresh and new in this moment. The past has gotten you here so it is done. Let it go. Breathe in this moment, experience it fully. And, look toward the future for what you desire next to manifest for your enjoyment.

Believe in fresh starts

*B*elieve in fresh starts. No one is so mired down that they can't begin again. No one is so lost that they can't let go and go with the flow. Allow yourself to take the gifts and experiences you have created for youself to the next place, level, or experience. Nothing is ever so bad in the past that you can't begin fresh and new in the present. For, this moment is all you can truly experience. Leave the past where it belongs, in your past. Appreciate it for having gotten you to today. Now, what will you do with your today?

Move with certainty

*M*ove with certainty. As you travel through your journey, and your day, move with certainty. Know that you are supported by countless nonphysical entities, helping to guide you to exactly where you've requested in your thoughts and desires. Each moment of each day is guided by supreme intelligence. Allow yourself to go with the flow. Allow yourself to be nudged along into exactly the correct place at the best possible time. All yourself, too, to enjoy each of these moments, for the more appreciation you show, the easier it is for us to know we are helping you along perfectly, and thus will be even more helpful. And, know you are loved beyond description and words by those like us in the nonphysical.

Move though life in joy

Move though life in joy. It is the goal, to be joyful as much and as often as possible, no matter what else is going on around you, no matter what anyone else thinks. The only emotional experience that matters is your own. You are not responsible for anyone else's emotions, and no one else is ever responsible for yours. So, since you're in absolute control at all times of your creation, why not strive to create joy as much as possible? Otherwise, you're simply making yourself miserable for absolutely no good reason.

Enjoy the opportunities

*E*njoy the opportunities. At each turn, the universe is presenting you with new opportunities. Each new opportunity is a time to feel a greater, happier, more love-filled emotion. Each opportunity is a new experience. Each opportunity is attracted to you through the divine Law of Attraction. So, take advantage of each new option. Use each experience to decide whether you want more of the same or something different. Know that you are aligning with each new opportunity because it is a step toward or closer to your creation, your manifestation of desire. This is your journey. What shall you do with it next?

Turn toward the sunlight

*T*urn toward the sunlight. Your sun shines constantly, providing light, energy, and a vast array of environmental positives to your earthly home. Turn toward this light, just as your planet does, just as the flowers and trees do. Spend time walking in the sunlight, resting in the sunlight. Eat foods nourished by the sun. Show your appreciation for the sun's presence.

Appreciate the air

Appreciate the air. Throughout your earthly home, the air permeates, brings life, and purifies. Breathe deeply of this precious resource. Show appreciation for its abundance. Appreciate the plants and trees that create it through their processes. Take time today to see the green plants and trees. Take time to look at and admire them. Offer a thought of appreciation for the part they play in your beautiful life.

Drink deep of the abundant waters

*D*rink deep of the abundant waters. Above you, near you, and below you, the waters of your earthly home are abundant. Don't seek out to create shortages, but instead know that there is a great abundance of this stuff of life. Know that with each passing day, more new technology is coming and arriving and thought up to clean, purify, and make available to all of you as much of this wonderful, abundant resource as you require. Take time today to appreciate the waters of your earthly home. They sustain life, including you. As you appreciate this source of life, you are creating more abundance for yourself and those around you.

Believe in your power

Believe in your power. You are the master creator of your emotional experience. So, focus on your emotions. When you feel better emotionally, everything thing else falls into place. You meet the right people at the right time, traffic flows for you, manifestations come for you. So, stop trying to create the manifestations. Let go of the to-do list. Focus your energy and intention on feeling great. Or good. Or, at least, better. Your emotions are your responsibility, your job. Everything else, well, the universe will take care of that.

You create the path you follow

You create the path you follow. You are always responsible for the creation of your life path. Each thought and desire leads to the inspiration of the next action to take. If you're enjoying your life much of the time, you're doing a great job. If you're not happy, then it's time to begin creating a more interesting and fun path for yourself. How? Start telling great stories. Tell great stories about where you are and where you're headed. Tell the stories to yourself and to anyone else around you. You'll soon be glad you did.

Follow your heart

*F*ollow your heart. Love and passion of life are essential to fining joy and happiness. Follow your heart toward your dreams. Follow your passion, it provides the steps of action that you must take to align with the manifestation of your dreams. Don't let others steer you away from your love and passion of life. They have nothing to do with your emotional journey. Only you know what your passions and dreams are leading you toward. So, follow your heart and follow your passions.

Find the joy in your life

Find the joy in your life. Each moment of your life is yours to command. You have the absolute power to feel anything you want. That is your greatest power and your only true control in this physical life. The better you feel, the more joyous you are, the greater and easier alignment you will experience. When you find and feel the joy in your life, your manifestations will begin to quickly align with you, without any additional effort on your part. So, reach inside of you and find joy. Find love. Find happiness. Find the best feeling thoughts and emotions you can and watch how your life rapidly improves to include your most desired manifestations.

Validation is all around you

*V*alidation is all around you. Each moment of your life is validation of where you are emotionally. Each moment is validation of your alignment with Source Energy and All That Is. Is this moment the best time you've ever had in your life? If so, good for you! If not, begin finding and aligning with joyful, love-filled emotions. As you feel better, or even great, striving toward joyful, the more fun you discover yourself having at every turn. Reach and strive and work toward feeling joyful. It is the answer you've been seeking.

Your best self is wherever you are

Your best self is wherever you are. You have created this moment. You create each moment in your life journey experience. Therefore, at any and every moment, you are the best you can possibly be. So, lighten up. Allow yourself to be on your journey. There's no such thing as perfection, only your ongoing and constant growth, expansion, and evolution. Know that you are a brilliant creator. Know that you can create for yourself anything you desire. And, know that, no matter what you've been told, or are even telling yourself, this moment offers the best you possible. As you desire more, as you desire different experiences, allow yourself to not only request and create them, but align with them through your knowledge that this moment is yours.

You hold all the power in your life

We wish to remind you, you hold all the power in your life. For, you are creating each experience you have. It's time that you take your power and use it to your best interest, not the interests of others. Yes, it's good to support others on their journey, but not at the expense of your own journey. Create for yourself that which you most desire without care of what others may think. Begin telling a story of how you are supported at every turn, not only by others, but by Source Energy and All That Is. And, since you create each moment, be mindful of your creation powers. Strive to create only that which you want. And, once you know it's created, strive to align with this creation. How do you know it's created? Just by thinking upon it you have created what you desire. How do you align with that creation? By knowing that it is done, it is created. Take time to enjoy life. Rest, relax, laugh, breathe deeply, and quiet your mind. This will allow the universe to bring into view that which you have created.

Follow where the path leads you

*F*ollow where the path leads you. We want to encourage you to gently and easily follow your path where it leads you. Look for inspiration and validation. Listen for hints and clues, both from within and from those you come into contact with. If you've been asking and creating, which you have, there's no way not to while you are in physical, there will be information, prompts, inspiration, and ideas coming to you however we, and those like us in nonphysical, can get them to you. So, quiet your mind. Be one with the universe. Listen and look for those moments of inspiration and ideas at every turn. Follow those wherever they lead you. That is the easiest and quickest path to aligning with that which you've created and that you most desire.

You're exactly where you're supposed to be

Y ou're exactly where you're supposed to be. You've created this moment. Revel in that creation. Ask for more of the same if you're enjoying your creation; ask for something different if you're not. Either way, know that this moment and each moment are your creation. You hold all the power and all the responsibility for each and every second of your life. Use this knowledge to your advantage. Don't expect anyone else to make it their job to make you happy. That's your job. And, likewise, it's not your job to make anyone else happy, that's their job. This is your creation, your journey. Enjoy it all you can.

Stop participating

S top participating. Stop reading negative stories. Stop complaining when others complain. Stop telling negative stories about your past or your present. Start knowing that you create each moment. Start knowing that your words and emotions are the tools that help you create your future. When you participate in negative thoughts, talking, reading, or viewing you are creating and calling more of that negative to you. Start telling great stories. Start seeing a brilliant, amazing future for yourself. Start calling to you only, and as much as possible, positive energy, stories, visions, and outcomes. You are the one with the power. How will you use it?

Being tuned in is easier than you make it

*B*eing tuned in is easier than you make it. When you're tuned in, you have access to all the knowledge of the universe. Through your tuning, you raise your vibration. During this time of heightened awareness, you will notice the arrival of information, intuition, synchronicities, and validation at just about every turn. And, you all make it so much harder than it needs to be. Simply learn to breathe deeply and quiet your mind. Then, just live your life, listening and looking for the clues, advice, aid, assistance, and knowledge that we, and those like us in nonphysical, are always bringing to you. Being tuned in is simply a heightened state of awareness. And, you can do it!

This is the world you've helped create

*T*his is the world you've helped create. It's time to stop being so critical of the world around you and to begin instead seeing it for the wonderful, amazing place that it is. Air, sunlight, water, they all are abundant. There are plentiful resources. And, there are amazing people all around you that help you to decide what it is you want to experience next. Take time today to appreciate your planet home. Be thankful and appreciative for those around you. And, know that your planet is never in peril. It is as you've created it.

There's no going back

There's no going back. Each personal journey, and this goes for every entity that exists, can only move forward. Appreciate your past, all aspects of it and all experiences, because your past got you to this very moment. There's no letting go of the past. There's no forgiveness required. The past has served its purpose. You've had the experiences the past provided and those experiences got you to this moment. And, you can only move forward. Any "issues" you have from the past, aren't really in the past, they're right here, in the present. And, as you dwell on those issues, you're simply asking for more of those emotional experiences. A better choice, by far, is to be in this moment and focus your energy and attention on the future you desire. Now, that's time well spent.

Love is more expansive than you know

*L*ove is more expansive than you know. As you expand your feelings of love, you expand all the possibilities in the universe. Know that all emotions along the entire scale of possible feelings are all based in love. For, you are here in physical because of love. You are always viewing yourself, that is your inner being, the true you, is always viewing yourself from a place of absolute and total love. Each moment and each breath are based in love. Each manifestation is based in love. Feel the great love that permeates through this entire universe. It is your true and base emotion. Reach and strive to feel as much love as you possibly can. And, as you feel this great love, you'll see your world around you reacting by bringing you more and more love.

Simply tap into the energy of the universe

*S*imply tap into the energy of the universe. There is brilliance at your fingertips. Simply tap into the amazing energy of the universe. Listen and look for the brilliant idea. Listen and look for each answer to each question you have. If you allow it, the universe will bring you all that you ask for and desire. It is your task to be open to this amazing flow of energy.

Be easy with yourself, and with others

Be easy with yourself, and with others. Don't be so hard on yourself. You are doing great. You're where you're supposed to be. You are loved on many dimensions. And, don't be so hard and judgmental of others. They, like you, are on their personal journey. The journeys of each of you are very personal and often don't make sense to anyone else. So, allow yourself to be on your personal journey. And, allow others to be on theirs. That's' the most supportive and loving thing you can do both for yourself and for others.

Your emotions are your responsibility

*Y*our emotions are your responsibility. No one can "make" you feel anything. You are always responsible for your own emotional experience. How you feel about anything or in any moment is totally and absolutely up to you. So, decide how you want to feel and reach for that emotion.

There is no end to your journey

There is no end to your journey. You may set goals and express your desires; those lead you along your journey. But, there is no end to that journey. You are an eternal being. When your time in physical is done, you shall emerge once again into source energy. You shall reap all the benefits of this latest physical journey, and all the growth and expansion of all the other journeys that have and are transpiring. So, take the time now to enjoy this journey as much as you can. It never ends, so there's no rush. Just take the ride. Allow the universe to provide the "how" of life. You simply get to enjoy the experience.

All is well

*A*ll is well. Everything is unfolding and evolving perfectly. You are, as always, exactly where you should be. This is the world you've created. This is the moment you've created. So, enjoy it as much as you can. Find as much joy as you possibly can. Take risks and chances. Live the life you most desire for yourself. This really is your moment.

Laugh more

*L*augh more. Laughing raises your vibration. Laughing releases tension and resistance. Laughing is fun. Laugh, Sing, Dance...celebrate your life and experience. Enjoy your friends and family. Have as much fun as possible. Create more joy in your life.

Surrender

*S*urrender. There's virtually nothing you have any control over, except your emotional experience. So, go with the flow of life, feel the emotions you feel, and decide how you want to feel next. Now, reach for your next emotional desire. The universe will take care of absolutely everything else.

Ease into the flow

*E*ase into the flow. All life is about a flow of energy. This great energy flow drives a continual forward motion into your physical lives. When you feel bruised and battered by your life experience, it is usually because you aren't going easily with the flow of this life-force energy. When you stop trying to control every moment of your day, and instead allow yourself to be open to the quick, easy flow, you will discover an ease of life. Your desires will come easily to you. Your emotions will be happier. You'll meet the right people at the right time. Traffic and lines will be flowing easily around you, inviting you to easily accomplish your daily tasks. Life is supposed to be as easy and as fun as possible. Allow it to be easy and fun for you.

There is a never ending flow of possibilities

There is a never ending flow of possibilities. With each experience, no matter how it turns out, you are setting new desires. There's a never ending stream of possibilities. So, take the path you most desire with the knowledge that there is always more for you to desire. Follow your heart, knowing there will always be even more path to follow. Take risks and chances for there is nothing that you can't have or do. This is your journey. Your experience. Your lifetime to do with as you please.

Be on your journey

Be on your journey. So many of you spend time thinking about or reliving the past. You so often worry about the future or what might happen. Live in this moment. Be in this moment. Enjoy this moment. This moment is, after all, your creation. Revel in your powers of creation, the creation that is being expressed and manifested right now.

Each moment is a new beginning

*E*ach moment is a new beginning. Because you are con-stantly creating the moments that you manifest and experience in your life, you can easily begin to think of each moment as a new beginning. It matters not what you've said, done, or thought in the past. It matters not how you arrived at this moment. This moment is a new beginning and you can now begin creating your future fresh from this point. If there are events, emotions, things, or people in your life right now that don't fully allow you the wonder of your life, it is okay to let them go and begin fresh creating what it is you truly want and desire. Nothing has been set in stone about your future. Your future is the story you are now tell-ing about it. So, tell the best possible story you can from this moment forward. That will, if you allow it, become your true future and destiny.

Don't follow; Lead

Don't follow; Lead. It is not your job to worry about others. It is not your job to follow the lead of others. It is your journey and you'd do well to allow yourself to take your own path where it leads you. Allow yourself to be on your journey. Allow others to be on their own journey. Enjoy the moments when these journeys merge and enjoy the moments when you are traveling alone. Your life is all about you and your own emotional experiences. So, have and feel everything and be on your own journey, be the leader you came here to be.

You are at the center of the universe

Y ou are at the center of the universe. Your world really does revolve around you. You are at the core, the center, the epicenter of your life experience. Start making your journey more about you than others. Follow your own inner guidance instead of the words and desires of others. This doesn't mean you can't be compassionate; being loving toward others is always good. But, you should never place the happiness of another before your own. This is, after all, your journey to do with as you most desire.

Begin believing in yourself

*B*egin believing in yourself. For most of your life, you've been told to have faith in others: in your family, your parents, your churches, your governments. None of this really matters. You will always align with where your personal vibration is set, and that's determined by your emotions and thoughts. It's time to begin having faith in yourself, the master creator of your experience. Begin fresh to believe in your amazing powers of creation. Know that you have created and aligned with every aspect in your current life. You hold all responsibility for where you are. So, take this moment to begin having faith in your own powers of creation. Begin raising your vibration toward love, joy, and happiness. Begin having faith that you truly can create and align with anything you desire. That's the knowledge to place your faith, trust, and knowing in.

You create the limits

Y ou create the limits. You set the boundaries. No one else can do this in your life, but you. You are the only one who can see your own horizon, or your own fences. Begin seeing larger, greater possibilities. Know that there truly aren't any limits for you except those that you create for yourself. See bigger. Dream bigger. Tell bigger stories about your future. And, allow those great outcomes to come to you by knowing they not only can, but do exist for you.

There's no such thing as negative energy

There's no such thing as negative energy. All energy flows from Source. Source Energy is pure love. Therefore, all energy is based in love. And, since everything is energy, everything is based in love. Know that all your emotions, no matter what they are at any moment, are based in the love of Source Energy. So, feel everything fully. Experience ever moment fully. And, bask in the love of Source Energy.

Know you're moving forward

*K*now you're moving forward. Forward is the only direction any of us move. Even when it doesn't feel like it, even when it feels as though you're stuck in place or even moving backward, this is never true. You are and always will be moving forward. Not only are you always moving forward along your personal path, you are doing so at a rather rapid speed. We understand that your perspective might not always reveal to you this fact, but your knowing it is important. And, we also wish that you know that you can't get it wrong, the choices you make are always helping you move forward along your journey. So, relax and be on your journey with absolute confidence that you're growing and expanding in perfect harmony with All That Is.

Expect joy in your life

*E*xpect joy in your life. Your thoughts, dreams, and yes, expectations create your future. Begin dreaming big. Begin consciously thinking positive thoughts. Begin expecting the best possible outcome for each of your endeavors. You can never expect too much. You can never dream too big. You can create and align with anything you desire. So, begin expecting your desires to manifest. Look joyfully around each corner for that which you expect.

Lighten up

*L*ighten up. So often, you all take yourselves too seriously. You take your positions on morality, politics, religion, education, society, and so forth way too seriously. Don't dig in on a position. Don't become rigid in your thinking. Allow the flow of energy to bring you new ideas, new concepts. Allow yourself to gently and easily change your opinions and ideals. There are no truths that are set in stone. Everything is and can always change. Every idea can become stronger. Every belief can be altered. Every truth you see and seek can change in an instant. Why? Because the universe, and the manifestations of your universe, are always expanding, changing, and growing. You'd do well to allow yourself to go with the flow of this expansion and change in a light, gentle, easy way.

Your power is immense

Your power is immense. You are the master creator of all your experiences. You are solely responsible for the experiences and emotions that you have. It's time to take this power to its fullest. It's time to feel fully. It's time to ask clearly for what you most desire. It's time to allow the flowing energy of the universe to run through you and to help you align with those creations, manifestations, and the emotions you most want to feel. This is your time. This is your power. Make the absolute most of it.

To believe in yourself is to believe in God

To believe in yourself is to believe in God. For, you are God. Not made in the image of another, but the maker of All That Is. You are the creator's creation and the creator of the creator. For, each thought you have, each emotion you express, each desire you manifest expands All That Is. You are God, plain and simple. And, through your journey, you are expanding God in all possible directions. Because you hold and are such power, never doubt your ability to create for yourself exactly the world you dream of and desire.

Don't be afraid to follow your passions

*D*on't be afraid to follow your passions. Inspired ideas and passions are what truly make life worth living. Don't be afraid to follow them wherever they may lead you. Don't be afraid of what others might think about you following your passions. You have not come forth into this physical life to please others. You have come forth to be on your own personal journey. You have come forth to expand and grow. This expansion and growth happen when you follow your inspired ideas and passions. Life is supposed to be fun and interesting. Life is about taking the journey and living the biggest life you can, filled with not only the biggest dreams possible, but to move toward and allow the manifestation of those great dreams in your life. So, follow your passions with the fullest intention and most open heart you possibly can.

You are here

Y ou are here. There's nothing more you need to do about the past. It got you here, to this moment. Now, it's time to create the future. If you have a desire you've already expressed, take a moment now to clearly see yourself having that experience. Otherwise, and in addition, create a new vision for your future that is the exact experience you desire most. Now, look for signs and validation because the universe is already doing all it possibly can to bring that desire to you. Allow us to do our part and begin to align with your desire right now.

You hold all the cards

Y ou hold all the cards. Life is a game and should be played for the fun of it. You hold all the cards. You create your reality. You create your future. You align with like-minded souls. You align with the vibration that best fits with your own. So, have fun. Dream big. Laugh as much as possible. And, in the process of that fun, you will more easily and quickly align with that which you have created for yourself.

Nothing can harm you

*N*othing can harm you. You create each moment in your life. So, create a life of happiness and wellbeing for yourself. See yourself healthy, well, and happy. Project joy and confidence. Know that the "risks" you take, are supported by the entire universe. Seek joy and wellness, expect joy and wellness, and you shall be happy and well.

Embrace the new

*E*mbrace the new. If you feel great and are having fun, then by all means, enjoy where you are and know that you're utilizing your master creator skills. But, if you're not living your life in joy and happiness, embrace the new. Get out of your comfort zone. Travel a new path. Follow a new idea. Begin listening to and following your passions. So often, those in physical get into a rut. You've gotten so used to your current emotional state that you don't see the other possibilities. The best, fastest, and easiest way to gain traction toward happiness is to break the cycles. Stop watching what you usually watch. Stop listening to what you usually listen to. Begin trying new things, even small ones. Change can come easily if you'll only begin something new, take a new risk, and follow your heart.

You'll get there.

Y ou'll get there. Each movement forward along your journey, and all movements are forward, takes you closer to aligning with your desires. Along the way, it is essential that you know in advance that you'll arrive at your desires. You must know, believe, and anticipate this alignment for it to happen.

We believe in you

We believe in you. Often, we believe in you more than you believe in yourself. As soon as you send out a request, no matter how big or how small, we, and those in nonphysical like us, begin taking care of all the moving parts to help you align with your creation. As soon as you ask, we create your desire. Not only do we create it, but we literally move heaven and earth to help you align. So, be open and look for signs that this is happening.

There simply are no limits

*T*here simply are no limits. We once again encourage you to dream bigger. You truly can have anything you desire, no matter what that something is. Dream it. See it. Know it exists for you. And, allow us to help you align with your desire.

Love the journey

*L*ove the journey. While we so often encourage you to dream big and align with your creations, the point of your physical life is to find and discover the joy of the journey itself. It matters not what you want or where you're headed, what truly matters is that you're having as much fun and enjoyment as possible on your journey. Find new ways to have fun and you'll quickly discover that you more easily align with your desires.

The stories you tell are yours to tell

*T*he stories you tell are yours to tell. You can tell any stories you want about how your life is going. We wish to encourage you to begin focusing and telling the stories about the things that are wonderful and working. We further encourage you, once again, to stop telling stories of the negatives in your life. Those perceived negatives, like the positives, are related to the vibration you create and align with. So, if you're telling negative stories, be ready for more negative experiences and emotions. Likewise, if you stick to the positive stories, if you love and laugh and enjoy the journey and talk about that, you'll get more and more of that vibration and thus more alignment with happy experiences. The choice is yours and you may do as you wish, always. But, the choice to be happy or not is also totally yours.

Revel in the choices you make

Revel in the choices you make. You can't get your journey wrong. You can't make a mistake. So, revel in the choices you make. Enjoy the direction you choose. And, if something isn't working, choose something new or different to focus upon. All the choices are yours. No one can make you do anything. Enjoy the journey.

This moment is simply the next step

*T*his moment is simply the next step. Your journey is ongoing and never ending. So, be in this moment. Enjoy this step along your path. There are many more steps ahead of you, no need to worry yourself about that. Be here. Be now. Breathe deeply and enjoy this moment as much as you possibly can. And, expect and know that the next step will also be a joyful one, and the step after that. Anticipate and expect happiness and joy and then begin to look for opportunities to enjoy the journey.

You are brilliant

You are brilliant. You are a brilliant creator. You have access to all the knowledge in the universe. Begin to listen and respond to your own intuition and knowing. Follow the great ideas and inspiration when they come to you. Believe that the answers to all of your questions are coming to you easily. For, this is how best to flow through life, tuned in to the vast universe.

Take some time for yourself

*T*ake some time for yourself. It is essential that you spend time quieting your mind. It is important that you spend time alone, doing things you enjoy. Walk in nature. Listen to your favorite music. Dance in your socks. Quieting your mind, loving yourself, and knowing yourself truly are essential to enjoying your life.

Breathe

*B*reathe. We thought we'd take this opportunity to once again remind you to breathe deeply. So often, those in physical simply forget to breathe consciously. So, take a moment now. Breathe deeply in on the count of three. Hold that breath for two counts. Now, release that same breath over a count of five. Repeat. Your mind will clear. Your blood will flow better. And, your vibration will be raised. It's just that simple.

Allow flow in your life

*A*llow flow in your life. Don't try or work so hard to manipulate and control all the moving parts and pieces of your life. Relax and allow us, and those like us, to help with all those moving parts. Don't take action until inspired. Don't force your way through your day. Instead, raise your vibration, ask for what you most desire, and know and trust that those desires, and all the pieces required of them, are being taken care of for you. You are loved and supported by more entities than you can ever count. Allow us to be at your service and to take care of the details.

Believe in magic

*B*elieve in magic. Magic is what so many refer to as the work of the universe. Those in nonphysical, like us and so many countless others, are always creating magic for you. This may come in little ways, number alignment on your clock (1:11, 5:55, etc.), all the traffic lights turning green as you approach them, etc. We also move bigger items around for you helping you meet the exact right person at the exact right time, bringing you validation and information as you align with your desires, and so on. This is what many of you call magic. This is simply asking for what you most desire and then allowing it to come to you with the aid of your guides, spirits, angels, and the countless other entities assigned to aid, help and assist you. How can you help? By believing in our magic. By allowing all the greatness that you desire. By seeing and knowing your absolute worthiness to receive all that you have created for yourself.

Try something new

*T*ry something new. So often you in physical find yourself in a rut. It may not be every aspect of your life that feels this way, but just one. When you're ready to move forward, when you're ready to allow change, try something new. It might be seeing the situation or person or emotion in a different way; it might be saying something in a new way; it may be deciding that you're going to feel different about the experience or emotion in a new way. The trick here is to do something different. Seek advice. Listen to your intuition. Take a break. Do some research. Do something new and different that you haven't tried before. Seek the next step toward something on your bucket list. Stand on your head or on your desk and view the world from that perspective. Change can't come if you always do the same things and always feel the same way. Breaking a pattern is one of the fast ways to have a new experience or a different take on a daily one.

What story are you telling?

What story are you telling? As you move through your day, be aware of the stories you're telling. Are you talking about the great, brilliant future you're headed toward, or about the negative thing that happened in your past? Are you telling stories of appreciation about the wonderful things that have happened to you or are you nagging and complaining about what this one did or didn't do? We encourage you to tell brilliant, uplifting, positive stories at all times. The past is done, it got you here. Every event of that past was your creation. If you're displeased with those outcomes, begin telling stories about the brilliant, creative, love-filled future you deserve and are worthy of. Your stories build your future. Tell great ones!

You are on an amazing journey

You are on an amazing journey. Never doubt that you are on an amazing journey. Each moment, each breath, each emotion, each experience is a special creation that you have both asked for and then aligned with. In between the asking and the aligning, we in Source Energy have taken care of all the "moving parts." So, ask for all you desire and know that we will also take care of those moving parts. Your only job or task is to discover the alignment with your latest creation. This is easiest when your vibration is high. So, reach for fun, reach for love, reach for joy, and know that that's the easiest and quickest way to align.

Allow more joy in your life

Allow more joy in your life. So often, you in physical grow very focused and serious about a given manifestation. We encourage you to lighten up. Know that life is supposed to be fun and joyful. You are here in physical to have fun. Sure, you're learning, growing, and expanding along the way. But, those are really secondary, or a byproduct. No, you're first goal should be to reach for the joy in life. Laugh, love, have fun, and enjoy all that you are creating. It's really the only true purpose of any journey.

Do you feel it?

Do you feel it? That's the energy of the universe flowing through you. That energy you feel is Source Energy, that which gives you life in physical. Do you feel it? Are you calling that life-force energy to you every moment of every day? Are you breathing deep and drawing as much as you can from the universe? Are you experiencing all you can? Are you loving all you can? If not, it's time. It's time for you to tap into the power of the universe and put that energy of Source to work for you. It's time to allow the power and flow of the universe to take care of all the moving parts and bring you that which you most desire.

Relax into it

*R*elax into it. As your vibration changes because of all the good work you're doing in this time and phase, relax into the experience. Allow change to come to you. Be open and willing to flow with the changing energy. Be gentle and have fun with this new, evolving, ever-changing you. This is the journey you asked for and created, so simply relax and enjoy it. You'll be pleasantly surprised at how easy everything truly can be.

Tune in

*T*une in. Whether you frequently tune in to the rhythm of the universe or it's new to you, this is the moment to tune in. There is a great awakening going on. More and more of you are coming to know the great energy and power of the universe. This isn't dependent on some religion, faith, or even the expertise of another. This tuning in is between you and that which you call God, Source Energy. The vast knowledge and experience of the universe is yours for the asking. It is yours for the taking. Simply tune in and allow the flow of Source Energy into your life.

You are the center of the universe

You are the center of the universe. Your whole world truly revolves around you. It is for you to choose and decide what you like and dislike about your world. In this choosing, you begin to change those aspects of your world. Now, allow those changes to take place. Know that you can't change the experience of another, only your own. Know that you can't alter another's journey, only your own. And, know that what another does has absolutely nothing to do with your own joy and happiness. It is up to you to align with those aspects of your life, as well as your creation.

Take control

*T*ake control. You hold all the control and responsibility in your life. Acknowledge this control. Know that you create every moment. Know that each emotion and experience is you aligning with the vibrational equivalent of where you are right now on your story, on your journey. You can only align with your vibrational equivalent. So, begin to do all you can to focus on only that which you desire and that which you desire more of. This is your power. This is your absolute control.

Each moment is a new beginning

*E*ach moment is a new beginning. It matters not what your past experience includes. It got you here, to to-day, to this moment. It is done. What matters is this mo-ment, this new beginning. Clean up your vibration. Start asking for what you want and desire. And, focus your energy on those wants and desires. You truly can have, be, or do anything you want. So, ask for what you want and then al-low the universe to take care of the moving parts. You'll be pleasantly shocked and surprised at how efficient we can be in getting you where you want to be if you'll only allow us to.

Your world is amazing and you are brilliant

Your world is amazing and you are brilliant. Stop your concern and worry about the end of your world. There isn't a cataclysm in sight. Your world is wonderful and safe. You are a brilliant master creator. But, even you aren't such a good enough creator to screw up your planet home. So, know you are well and safe. Know your planet home is well and safe and will be a place called home by humans and many other creatures for longer than you can imagine. Doesn't it feel good to know this? And, now that you are in the know, go out and spend your time creating that which you most desire instead of that which you fear most.

Where's your focus?

Where's your focus? You get what you think about. You manifest what's closest to your current vibration. Whatever you focus on sets your vibration. So often, the physical human's focus is on the missing, or the lack in their lives. It is time to begin to focus on your desires. It is to begin focusing on what you want, and not worrying about the how of that focus. Let us help you. Know and believe that that which you focus upon is coming to you. We will bring you together with all the moving parts in subtle and not so subtle ways. So, focus your focus on your greatest desires and the joy the manifestation of those desires will bring to you.

Look for validation

*L*ook for validation. As you tune in more frequently to the energy of the universe, expect to see and look for signs of validation. These may come in fun, little ways, like all the numbers on the clock aligning (5:55, 11:11, etc.), or all the lights turning green as you approach them in your car. They may come in silly ways, like when you mention something you want, say a trip to Hawaii, and everywhere you turn are information and images about that desire. Validation can also be great, such mas meeting exactly the right person at exactly the right time, or enjoying a financial windfall just when you need it most. These coincidences are you aligning with the energy of the universe.

Are all the traffic lights red for you? That's nothing more than a slight indication and nudge that it's time to quiet your mind, meditate a bit, laugh a little more, worry a little less, and go more with the flow of the universe as you travel through your day than you have been.

Are you hungry for more?

*A*re you hungry for more? If you're doing it right, being a human that is, you'll always be hungry for more. More love, more life, more experiences, more emotions. Sure, there are always more material manifestations, too. Are you desires strong? Is your journey exciting to you. Is each moment more exciting than the last one? If so, you're doing this life thing "right." Of course, no matter what your experience, you can't actually get it wrong, for each experience helps you expand, grow, and desire. But, having great desires, one after the other after the next is the way we recommend you live your life experience. Want more. Feel more. Love more. Laugh more. More. More. More. That's really the whole point to living in physical. So, have the ride and experience everything as fully as you can.

You are loved!

Each moment is perfection

*E*ach moment is perfection. Whether you're joyous and happy or not, this moment is perfection. You have created it; it is filled with source energy. It took an amazing number of moving parts to create this moment that you requested. Be joyous about its manifestation. Allow the energy of this moment to flow over you and feel all the emotions about this moment that exist for you. Now, what will you do with the next moment? What will you create for yourself next? Decide how you want to feel. Decide what you want in your life, emotionally and materially. See it. Focus on it. Allow it to come to you. That is Law of Attraction, the true law of your universe.

Your experience expands everything

*Y*our experience expands everything. Each moment you experience, each emotion you experience, and each physical manifestation you experience expands the collective knowledge of the universe. It also actually expands the universe because your experience expands All That Is, Source Energy. You have come forth into a physical form to be on the leading edge of creation and expansion. It is your chosen role and it was your desire before your physical manifestation. Embrace this important role by dreaming big, feeling everything, and allowing the flow of energy that propels you forward on your journey. This journey of expansion is supposed to be fun for you, so allow it to be.

Angels are around you

*A*ngels are around you. Know that your angles and guides are always around you. They gladly focus where you focus and take care of the moving parts for you. There's little required of you but to go through your day knowing you are supported, loved, and aided by those in nonphysical. They are always helping you to manifest exactly what you've asked for and requested, whether you've done so consciously or unconsciously. So, know we have your back and align with that which you've created.

You've chosen this life

Y ou've chosen this life. Before you arrived in physical you chose the set up for the journey. You selected your parents and agreed to your siblings. Once here, you've created each and every moment through conscious and unconscious thought. Three are no victims in life. There aren't any options for regrets. You hold all the cards, all the responsibility. So, enjoy this journey. Embrace those around you. And, create the next moment and the one after that with forethought and intention...or not. It's all up to you and it always has been.

Step forward with confidence

S tep forward with confidence. We're with you each step of your journey. We enjoyed the journey you've taken so far; it has expanded All That Is and Source Energy. And, we are already enjoying the next steps you'll take. You've asked and we've already moved forward to call and guide you to the place you've requested. So, take the next step with confidence. You can't get it wrong, for you are always perfection.

You can't go backward

Y ou can't go backward. Never be concerned that you are falling back into old habits or moving backward in any way on your journey. No matter what happens, you are always moving forward. When it feels like you've stepped backward, know that this is simply you creating by default, out of old habits of creation. Take those moments, those backward feelings, as an indication that it's time to begin once again to consciously create the future you desire.

There are no setbacks in life

There are no setbacks in life. Each moment is your creation. Each moment is also your opportunity to ask for what you most desire next. So, if you don't like this moment, ask for that which you desire more. Don't view things that happen as a negative. Show your appreciation for each moment because it is more clearly helping you define that which you most desire next.

Allow change

*A*llow change. If you've been requesting new desires, allow the change that is offered and suggested by the universe. Isn't it obvious? Changes and new opportunities are part and parcel of aligning with those new desires. It's virtually impossible to align with the new manifestations that you've requested if you're doing the same old things, following the same old routines. Allow change. Follow your inspired thoughts. Talk to the new people you meet. Click on those links when you feel inspired. Try new menu items. Go to new places when inspired. Doing so will help and aid you in more quickly aligning with your newest and latest creations.

Allow others to be on their journeys

A llow others to be on their journeys. Each of you has come into physical to have your own collection and set of experiences. Through these experiences you grow, expand, and hopefully align with your own happiness. Do not judge the journey of another. They are doing their thing, as it should be. You are doing yours. Know that if you're aligning with others who you choose to judge harshly, that this is your alignment with your own creation. As you point out the perceived flaws in others, you are actually asking the universe to provide more people whose flaws you can point out. Instead, begin pointing out the happiness and success in others, this will attract more happiness and success into your own experience.

You are worthy

Y ou are worthy. No matter what anyone has ever told you or you have ever thought, you are worthy. You deserve to have all that you desire and you are worthy of having it. There is no one in the universe more powerful or important than you are. No one! This is your journey. You are here filled with divine energy. You are an extension of All That Is, of God. And, by this extension, this makes you God. So, know your worth. Be thrilled and excited by the options and possibilities in your life. And, by all means, no matter what anyone ever says to you again, know that we know and believe that you are worthy of being here in physical, and worthy of all you desire and can imagine for yourself.

Each moment is a new beginning

*E*ach moment is a new beginning. There's no need to look back. Allow this moment to be the new beginning that it is. At every turn, you have the opportunity to begin creating with intent. You can let go and leave behind all that is not working with a deep breath and a moment of appreciation for the past having gotten you safely to today. Now, know that you can have anything you want, the way you desire it. It really is that simple.

Be your own frontrunner

Be your own frontrunner. No one else really matters but you. You're on a wonderfully selfish journey where it really is all about you. Yes, you do co-create with others at times, but the emotional experience is always yours. How you feel and react is always on you. No one else can create or feel your emotional experience. So, begin putting your own emotions first. Reach always for the best feeling thought. Know that the only one responsible for your own happiness is you. What will you do to improve your emotional experience today?

Feel what you're feeling

Feel what you're feeling. You've arrived at this moment with an emotion. How does it feel to be here right now? How does it feel to be you in physical right now? This is your launching off point. Do you like this feeling? This moment? If so, rejoice. Dance in your socks. If you can feel better, happier, more loving, more joyous than you do right now, then by all means, reach for that better feeling thought. Be on your emotional journey with as much desire as you can muster toward feeling as good as possible. That's what really matters most.

Move on

M ove on. Let it go. Whatever that thought or emotion is that's been holding you in the past, let it go. Learn to appreciate all your experiences. They got you to this moment. Become more and more aware that you can and will create the next moment and all those that follow, whether you're doing so with intention or not. So, let go. Declare your intentions. Fly. Soar. Be one with your flow of universal energy.

It is done

*I*t is done. Know that that which you have requested has been created. It is done. Now, get on with the allowing. Don't get so caught up in the asking that you continue to ask and ask and ask. The manifestation you desire is at a different vibrational place than the request. So, if you stick to the vibration of the request, you can't align with the manifestation of the creation. You would do well now to begin "working" on your aligning. How? Stop thinking, obsessing, worrying about the creation or how the manifestation will come, or where it is at this moment. Live your life. Do fun things. Laugh and love. Walk in nature. Relax. Enjoy your journey. As you do so, you will begin to see signs of validation that you're on the right track. And, with those signs, know that you are moving closer and closer to aligning with your desires.

There's always more

*T*here's always more. You live in an abundant universe. There is never really a shortage of anything you desire, least of all love and peace. So, dream big. Ask for what you most desire. And, know that you're having the manifestation is never keeping another from having what they desire. You are worthy of your wants. And, if you ask clearly and focus with intention, you can manifest anything.

Gently follow your dreams

Gently follow your dreams. Gently follow your passions. There's plenty of time. There's absolutely no rush to this lifetime, or any of your lifetimes. You can never get it all done. So, instead of rushing around trying to do all and be all, just simply be as you gently and easily follow your passions and dreams. The fun part of this is that the easier you are about achieving that which you desire, the easier that which you desire can come to you.

You are responsible

You are responsible. You are always responsible for your own feelings. No one else can ever "make" you feel anything; your feelings are yours. By the same token, the feelings of others are theirs. Nothing you do, say, or think can transfer the responsibility of feelings. So, make it your top priority to feel the way you feel, take responsibility for those feelings, and, if you desire a different feeling, don't expect others to change. It must be you that alter your thinking, actions, deeds, and thoughts. Do whatever it takes for you to feel better.

The flow of energy never stops

*T*he flow of energy never stops. Don't ever think you've gotten so far off your path that you're out of the flow. The energy of the universe is constantly flowing and pulsing through you. You are always connected through this flow to infinite intelligence. You can do anything at any moment. So, know you're exactly where you're supposed to be in this perfect moment. Know the vast power of the universe is not only at your beck and call, but actually within you right now. And, take the next step toward that which you desire.

Have you discovered how easy it is?

*H*ave you discovered how easy it is? Life is supposed to be easy and fun. This doesn't mean that there won't at times be challenges and contrast to work through. But, even the process of working through challenges should actually remind you how easy life in physical can be if you decide it will be. You hold all the power. You hold all the control. All of it. Over everything. So, begin knowing and allowing your life to be easy and it will quickly become easier. It's the greatest "secret" of all the ages. Life is only difficult when you choose to allow it to be so. Be easy and allow your life to be easy, too.

What's next for you?

What's next for you? What is it you want next? What dreams do you have? What desires have you been thinking about? Get the picture. Go as big as you can. Enjoy a vision as clear as you can, so long as it still feels good to you. Now, know that your dream, your desire has been created. Follow the passion and focus as it comes to you without concern or worry for the how of it. We will lead and call you right to your desire.

Don't push against things

*D*on't push against things. The quickest way to get more of anything is to focus your attention upon it. So, when you desire something new, spend time focusing on how wonderful it will be to have what you desire. See it, feel it, know it. Likewise, when there's something you don't want more of, or something you want changed, don't focus on it as it is now. Don't spend time pushing against it or protesting it. Instead, focus on how it can be, how you desire it to be. Either way, you're going to get what you focus on.

Each moment is yours

*E*ach moment is yours. You may do with them as you wish. If you want to live actively and create with intention, so you may. If you choose to simply drift along and see what comes your way to react to, you certainly can do that. If you wish to stubbornly hold on to the past, with all its actions and memories, that, too, may you do. It is up to you how you spend your time here in physical. You can't get it wrong, for all your choices and dreams help you grow and expand. Will you take the thrill of that growth and expansion now, in this moment? Or, will you do what so many do, wait until you transition out of physical, back to purely nonphysical, to enjoy the fruits of your experiences here in physical. The choice really is yours. It always has been and always will be.

Your world is perfection

Your world is perfection. Stop looking and seeing only the things you do not prefer. Look for the things you like. Either way, whatever you focus on, you'll get more of. That's how this all works.

There is no competition

*T*here is no competition. Each of you is unique. Your thoughts and creations are unique. You align with those interested in your message at each moment. There is no competition of any kind. Only alignment. Know you are aligning perfectly at all times both with your message and your audience.

This IS your journey

*T*his IS your journey. Stop looking so far down the road, out in front, and behind you to the past. You are here, right now, on your journey. This is it. Yes, it's good to ask and expect what you desire. But, the real point of living in physical is to be in the moment, to experience the emotions of the now, of this very moment. So, feel the journey. Know where you are at this very moment. Breathe deeply and have the experience of being on the physical journey.

Create your own beliefs

Create your own beliefs. It matters not how you were raised or what others have expected you to believe in. Your beliefs are your own. They can be anything you want them to be. And, beliefs are meant to be changed over time, as you grow and expand, as you experience life, your beliefs can and should alter. So, see where you are today and decide what you believe in at this moment. Live with those beliefs for a bit and see how they feel. Then, alter and change as necessary to maintain your own happiness.

Feel fully

*F*eel fully. It matters not what you're feeling, you can't get feelings wrong. So, feel whatever it is you feel. Embrace each emotion. Decide if you want more of the same or something different to feel. Now, begin feeling the next moment.

You can't get it wrong

Y ou can't get it wrong. You simply can't get anything wrong. Each experience is just that, an experience. If you did it and it feels good, then do more of it. If you did something and it didn't feel good, then don't do that again. Neither of these experiences are right or wrong, they're just experiences.

The sky is the limit

*T*he sky is the limit. Begin dreaming bigger. This doesn't necessarily mean you should only desire physically large things, but rather the absolute best feeling thoughts and emotions related to that which you most desire. It's time to start feeling better and enjoying your life more, whether you are manifesting or not. It's really one of the points of being in physical, to enjoy the experience as much as possible and to move from whatever you are feeling to the best possible emotion you can attain.

What are you waiting for?

*W*hat are you waiting for? There is no better time than now to become you. Don't hide or shield yourself from anything. Allow each experience to happen fully so that you can more clearly define that which you most desire next for yourself. Be yourself. Speak your truth. Allow yourself to grow fully. Experience all that you can. Have as much fun as possible. Be who you are, not who others expect you to be or who you think you should be. Just be you, now.

You're the only leader

Y ou're the only leader. The only person for you to follow is you. The only entity for you to emulate is you. You are the most powerful person in your life. You hold all the cards. You hold all the creation. Each moment is yours and you are beholden to no one else for your experience and outcomes. So, be bold. Lead yourself with strength and power. You are the master creator of your own experience.

Feel emboldened

*F*eel emboldened. There's nothing you can't have or create for yourself. Feel emboldened to be yourself; speak with your true voice; create everything you desire; and, freely walk your own journey without worry or concern for others. Allow yourself and others to be on your own personal, selfish journeys with joy and love.

Your journey is perfect

Your journey is perfect. Each moment of your physical journey is your personal creation and manifestation. There is absolute perfection in each of the moments you experience. Begin to appreciate them as you decide if you want more of the same or something different to experience next.

Be allowing

*B*e allowing. Allow yourself to be yourself. Allow others to be themselves. Don't expect anyone else to make you happy. It's not their responsibility. Likewise, it's not your responsibility to make anyone else happy. Be on you r journey. Allow your manifestations to align with you. Support others on their journey by allowing them to be on them.

Step into the light

Step into the light. Spend time in the shade. Experience each temperature. Smell all the flowers. Commune with the animals. Appreciate all the insects. Each creation, whether you're aware of them or not, is helping to balance your perfect planet home. Take a moment to appreciate that this happens without your having to consciously spend time each moment creating it. Perfection is done.

Your guides are with you

*Y*our guides are with you. Whether you are consciously aware of them or not, your team of guides and angels is always with you. They are offering information, answers, guidance, and love at all times. Your spirit guides and angels never offer negative thoughts or judgment. They always come with you with all the love available from Source Energy, which is only a place of love. Know you are loved and supported, always.

This is your world

*T*his is your world. You create each moment and experience you have while in physical. Know fully that this is your world. Begin creating that which you most desire by first dreaming it, then believing your dream exists, and finally allowing yourself to align with your own creation. While you can't create in the experience of another, you certainly can create within your own experience. So, get busy.

Breathe

*B*reathe. As is our want, we once again remind you to take some time and breathe deeply and with conscious intention. Ground yourself in your body and in your worldly realm. Breathe deep to allow the flow of energy to travel more easily through you. Breathe deeply to help you quiet your mind. Breathe deeply to appreciate the wonder that the human physical body is. Breathe deeply.

Be on your way

*B*e on your way. A great deal is made by many of spirituality and creation. It really is time to spend a little less time thinking and a little more time being. Be conscious of your life. Be conscious of your surroundings. Be conscious of your emotions. Be conscious of your experiences. This is your journey. It's why you're here. Sure, you can take some quiet time each day, a few minutes, and contemplate nonphysical. But, you're here in physical to experience the physical world. So, live in the moment. Feel in the moment. Be in the moment. Revel in the moment.

Tune in more often

*T*une in more often. We, and those like us who support you from our nonphysical place, have a vast amount of information and energy to offer you. All you need do is quiet your mind and tune in to us to begin taking greater advantage of what we have to offer you.

Try something new

*T*ry something new. So often, the rut you find yourself in comes from doing the same, repetitive things over and over. It comes from thinking the same thoughts over and over. It's time to break free of your patterns, both your patterns of thoughts and your patterns of action. Try something new. It could be something huge or something small. Just do it. It's time.

Beliefs change

*B*eliefs change. With each moment you live in physical you are changing your beliefs. There are not, nor were there ever meant to be, any beliefs that are so set in stone that they can't be changed. For, after all, even stone is always changing, whether you notice those changes or not. Allow change in your life and you'll find in short order that you are happier. Go with the flow of your new thoughts. Believe what seems appropriate in the moment. Don't align yourself with the beliefs of others, but instead believe your own ideas. It's time.

Go with the flow

Go with the flow. You've spent a lot of time, consciously or unconsciously, creating your now and your future. So, lighten up a bit, go with the flow, and see what your creation brings to you. Then, gently assess where you are, what you want next, and then set your new desires and intentions. You're making this all much more difficult than it needs to be, or than you want it to be. Breathe. Go with the flow. Allow us to help you align with your desires. (And, anything else you've created for yourself.)

The universe is ever expanding

The universe is ever expanding. All you do, all you think, each breath you take, each moment you're in physical expands the universe. All That Is and Source Energy become greater because you are in physical. You are the most important entity that exists. Embrace this knowing. Live more fully. Enjoy the journey as much as possible. And, know that you are worthy of all you dream and desire.

Get excited

Get excited. Life is supposed to be fun. You're supposed to be as excited and as passionate about all that you do as you possibly can be. So, follow your passions. Look for opportunities to have fun. Expect excitement at all moments of your day.

Allow change

*A*llow change. You are always changing. With each new experience and each new emotion, you are growing and expanding with the universal change you are helping to create. So, allow yourself to change. That which you believed yesterday might not be relevant today. Go with the flow. See change. Allow change. And, allow yourself to be fully on this wonderful journey.

Spirituality is becoming the new normal

Spirituality is becoming the new normal. As more and more of you in physical begin to open to the energy of the universe, the "new" concepts of spirituality are being embraced. Of course, these are really old concepts, not new ones. But, we're glad they're reemerging as important. What are these concepts? Everything is spirituality; everything is spiritual. There's no single or one way to be spiritual. For, there is a unique spirituality for each entity now in physical.

Everything is spiritual

*E*verything is spiritual. Everything in physical is a manifestation. Manifestations are thoughts before they become physical realities. All thought is based on belief. Movement of energy has a life force component that is Source Energy. That energy is spirit. All things in life, in existence, are based in spiritual beliefs and knowings. All manifestations are extensions of spiritualty. So be. Embrace fully your life experience. Know that you are a spiritual manifestation of your own thoughts and beliefs.

Relax

*R*elax. Relax into the experience of being you. Be easy and gentle about the experience of others around you. Relax and be easy about your emotions. Feel what you feel, but know your emotions are little more than a simple indicator of where you are on your journey. Just relax. Do the things you most enjoy without concern for the thoughts, deeds, or actions of others. Just relax and do all you can to enjoy your own journey.

There's always more

*T*here's always more. No matter how far you have come, there's always more to experience. No matter what your journey has been, there's always more to feel. No matter what science or organized religion says, there is always more to learn, grow, and expand. Your journey is never ending...and amazing. Know: There's always more.

Fly free

*F*ly free. You own nothing to anyone. The only opinion that matters is your own. There is no god to answer to, only your present self. You can't get anything wrong. You are always perfect and exactly where you're supposed to be because you created this moment you're living. Embrace your journey. Embrace your emotions. Embrace your power of creation and manifestation. This is YOUR journey and you are beholden to no one.

Time is only perspective

*T*ime is only perspective. Your concept of time is only a personal perspective. Yes, many of you have chosen to create a system of time related to your plant's movement around and with the sun. But, time is easily warped, altered, and molded to fit your own experiences. How many times has it seemed that time slows or speeds up for you? How often you say "time stopped." Or your vision/perception went into slow motion. It is your perception of time that does this, speeds, slows, etc. So, if you find you don't have enough time, stop telling that story and begin telling a story that there is always plenty of time. Likewise, if you feel time is moving too slowly, then begin telling a story of how quickly time passes. You are just as in control of time as you are every other aspect of your physical existence.

You are God

Y ou are God. That which you perceive as your inner being in nonphysical, your nonphysical self, that is what you humans think of as God. Yes, there is something greater than you here in physical, it is your nonphysical being. And, yes, there is "something" greater than that. You are part of the collective whole of the energy of the universe. That is what we mean when we say "All That Is" or "Source Energy." But, the entity that you pray to (and that hears your prayers), that is your inner being. Your inner being, the nonphysical you, is your direct connection to All That Is and the vast energy of the universe and beyond.

Travel your journey

*T*ravel your journey. You would do well to begin traveling your journey and not the journey others have prescribed for you. It does little good to only worry about making others happy. You're missing out on your own happiness if you're putting the wants and needs of others first. You come first on your list of priorities. This is your own personal journey you are currently on. So, be bold. Accept responsibility for your life and actions. And, be on your own journey.

Lighten up

*L*ighten up. Laugh. Play. Have as much fun as possible. And, by all means, lighten up. There's no actual requirement to take anything seriously, including your concepts of God and religion. Those of us in nonphysical are having a great amount of fun at all times. We exist in a state of bliss. And, while having all sorts of emotional experience is one of the points of being in physical, there's no real need to spend too much time in the muck....just enough to know you prefer something better.

Find the joy

*F*ind the joy. No matter what the situation or experience, there is always joy to be found, or discovered. If you're not feeling it, and we certainly hope you are, take the time to look for and discover the joy in all that you do, feel, and encounter. For, if you're doing something that is without joy, we must seriously ask you, "Why?" Life is supposed to be joyful and fun.

Take action when inspired

*T*ake action when inspired. There is little to no point of taking action toward your goal until you feel inspired to do so. When you ask for something or want something or desire something, the universe immediately creates that experience or opportunity for you. It then begins helping you to align with the vibration of the new desire. Searching and acting toward that desire without alignment is like hunting for a needle in a haystack. Instead, wait for the universe to help you align by only taking action when you feel inspired to do so. And, if you're not yet feeling inspired, don't force it. Instead, spend some time meditating and/or doing the things you already enjoy. The process of arriving at your desires should be easy and enjoyable. If it's not, you're working too hard.

Allow more flow

Allow more flow. The energy of the universe, Source Energy, is flowing around and through you at all times. Ease up just a bit on your worry and doubts. Releasing this resistance will allow an easier flow of this amazing energy. And, when the energy is flowing easily, that which you desire can manifest much more quickly.

Be you

Be you. Be the person you feel yourself to be. Be in the moment. Be god. Be the flower or the tree. Be one with the universe. Be one with yourself. Be happy. Be sad. Be joyous. Be angry. Be the emotional physical human you wanted to be when you arrived in physical. Be an explorer. Be a follower. Be a leader. Be a student. Be a teacher. Be. Just be. Be you in the moment. Feel everything. Think everything. Try everything. Be. Just be you in this moment.

Feel everything

*F*eel everything. Feel your emotions. Feel the physical sensations that come with being human. Feel the energy around you. Feel the energy flow through you. Feeling everything helps you ask for that which you desire next, that which you most want and desire to feel next. Physical sensation adds to your emotional sensation. So, feel fully, the gamut of possible physical sensations.

Opinions matter not

O pinions matter not. Live your life. Be on your journey. Don't do that to please others, but rather to please you. Your world revolves around you. You get to decide what to do next. Don't do it to please others. Please yourself first. You are at the top of your own priority list. So, live your life without concern for the opinions of others. Find that place within you that understands and knows that your opinion is the only one that matters for your own journey.

Focus

*F*ocus. That's how to align. That's how you create. That's how you journey with intention. Focus. You can choose to focus on anything you want or desire. You can choose to focus on anything you don't really want or desire. But, know that whatever you do choose to focus upon, for whatever reason, you will surely receive more of because that is how this brilliant universe works. That's the design. Like attracts like. That which you focus your energy and attention upon, you shall receive.

Follow your heart

*F*ollow your heart. It has been a while since we've reminded you to follow your heart. It is no less important today than it was the previous times. Follow your heart. Do what feels right and good to you. Follow your passions, for those are always right. Follow the path you yourself have created. If a choice feels good, do it. If a thought feels good, think it. It is that feeling in your heart that is the constant indicator of where you are. When things feel good to you, they are the right choice, always. So, take time today to listen to what your heart is telling you and then follow where those emotions lead you.

There's nothing required of you

*T*here's nothing required of you. You may choose to do anything you desire. You don't have to satisfy any god or religion while you are here in physical. The only "person" or entity that you must answer to is yourself. This is difficult for others to understand, but you are the creator of your destiny, as well as each moment of your physical existence. You hold all the power, completely. So, joyfully be on your journey.

Be patient where you are

Be patient where you are. You have created this moment. You create each moment. Be patient in that moment you've created. Feel it. Experience it fully. Be in the now of that moment. And, as you're fully experiencing your creation, decide if you desire more of the emotion you're feeling or if you'd rather feel a different emotion. In this moment of choosing, you are creating a future moment for yourself. Now, begin the process of aligning with the new moment by knowing it is coming and allowing it to come to you. Usually, you do all of this creation without a thought for it, just like you rarely think about your breathing. But, like breathing, when you breathe consciously and deeply it is better for your body, so thinking consciously about your emotional state and your creations, can improve your manifestations.

You create the rules

*Y*ou create the rules. You create all the rules that you play your life by. You are responsible for each thing, action, thought, deed, emotion, and experience you have. You don't have to play the game of life by any rules other than those you create. Just because so many others decide to create rules doesn't mean you are expected to or required to play by them. That, like everything else in your life, is your personal decision.

There is nothing more for you to do

There is nothing more for you to do. There are no expectations or requirements from a being or entity greater than you. There's nowhere you're supposed to be. There's nothing you are required to do. You are not working off karma from some past life. There is no one outside of yourself for you to please, attempt to please, make happy, or even really care about. Everything that happens while you are in physical is your creation; is for your own growth and expansion; is an expression of yourself and your perceptions; and beyond all, is for your entertainment, joy, fun, love, and amusement. This really is your journey. You chose it. You are experiencing it through your feelings. This is yours, and only yours. Now, what will you do next?

Allow yourself to be

A llow yourself to be. You are here, now. You have lived a great journey to arrive at this moment in time. Take at least one moment today to appreciate that you have arrived here. Take one moment to just be, to just exist. Feel this moment. Be in this moment. Appreciate this moment.

Find your passions

Find your passions. Find your joy. Be excited. Do the things you want to do without care of the opinions of others. Be on your own journey. Have your own fun. Let others be on their journey while you are on yours. It is time to begin enjoying life for all it's worth.

What an amazing journey

What an amazing journey. Be on it. Enjoy it. Appreciate it. Wallow in the emotions of it. Wreck yourself. Love yourself and others. Go for the thrills. Enjoy the chills. Experience all and everything that you possibly can. It's not that you'll only get to do this once. You get to reincarnate as often as you desire. No, it's about having the most amazing experiences you possibly can this time around because it's fun and amazing to do so.

Allow everything

*A*llow everything. You are resting currently at a vibration. All that you are aligning with has a direct relation and connection to that vibration you're resting at. If you want to align with something else, you must alter or allow your vibration to be altered. Usually, the experiences and emotions you truly want and desire are at what you in physical consider to be a higher vibration. So, to more easily allow that which you desire to come to you, "raise" your vibration. Sounds so easy, right? And, it is. Simply mediated, spend time in nature, laugh, sing, dance, or do anything else that you truly enjoy. Spend a little time appreciating how good you're feeling when you're doing the things you love to do. This will allow more to come to you, more to manifest, more of what you desire to align with you.

Allow brilliance

*A*llow brilliance. When you tune in to source, you are brilliant. When you allow the flow of energy from the universe through you, you are brilliant. When you allow your passion and creativity to flow to the surface, you are brilliant. All connections and feelings of those connections to source Energy are brilliant. You are and always have been brilliant. So, allow yourself to be brilliant.

Feel everything

*F*eel everything. Feel each and every moment to the fullest. Feel everything to the fullest. Be emotional. Let go of stoicism. If you feel it, it matters. It's important. Be in the moment. Feel in the now. Feel fully and without guilt, fear, or explanation to others. your feelings are yours. They are your experiences. Feel fully what you feel.

Know all is well

*K*now all is well. No matter what you feel at this very moment, in the greater, grander, larger picture of the universe, all is well. Each moment and experience you have, whether it feels good to you or not, is serving the express purpose of expanding All That Is, of adding to the collective consciousness, and of expanding the universe. While we'd prefer for you to have an enjoyable, fun journey, in the end, however you choose to experience physical, joyfully or not, is helping out, expanding, adding to, and generally improving the state of collective consciousness. So, be on the journey you choose. Do it joyfully, or not. Have fun, or don't. Love, or don't. It's all totally up to you. It's your responsibility and your choice how you feel and how much love, fun, joy, and opportunity that comes through your life experience.

Create with clear intent

Create with clear intent. Tell clear stories of that which you desire. Be clear and concise as you can. As we, and those like us, help you align with your desires, feel free to tell better stories, stories with more clarity and intention. Life is about experiencing manifestation and deciding if you want more of the same or something different. So, begin telling a new story based on where you are and what you now want. If you are at a loss, be vague; and, as you know more clearly what you desire, add more detail and intention.

Be yourself

*B*e yourself. It's just that easy. Be yourself. Follow your heart. Say what you're inspired to say. Feel all your emotions fully. Find and discover and create as much joy, happiness, love, and fun as you possibly can. Just be you on your journey. There isn't anyone else to please or make happy. There is no one to answer to ever except you in this moment. Be yourself, always.

It's just another day

*I*t's just another day. Yes, it is a magnificent co-creation, this day you're now experiencing. Yes, the energy of God flows through this day, through you, through all of creation. Yes, you are a magnificent creator yourself who has created this fine moment you're experiencing. Yes, you have absolute control over how you feel in this very exquisite moment. You can see it for the grand, beautiful gesture that it is, that Source Energy sees it as, or you can be miserable and bitchy. You can be anywhere in between. Yes, it's just another day, just another perfect manifestation. How are you going to react to it?

Begin anew

Begin anew. Each day is a new and fresh opportunity to create the life you most desire. Begin anew today to consciously and with intent begin creating the life and experiences you most want and desire. See your future, not the one that currently exists, but the nearly perfect one you actually desire. See it with details. Smell it. Feel it. Touch it. Hear it. You are the story teller of your life. Begin telling the story of your desired life. Begin anew.

Tell simpler stories

*T*ell simpler stories. Telling a simpler, easier, less complicated story is a sure way to begin moving energy in a new way. You don't have to let go of what you want, just begin telling an easier story. We and the universe don't need or require every little detail of why you want something and how you want it. Simply let us know what you desire in the most simple and basic terms and let us bring it to you. The truth is that your inner being already knows every detail perfectly. So, relax and let us do our work. And, remember that the question and the answer (the request and the receiving) are different vibrations.

You are loved

You are loved. It is always a solid reminder to experience: You are loved. There are so many entities that love and support you from our nonphysical vantage point. In fact, each and every individual in nonphysical loves and supports you. Each of us believes in you. Each of us want you to have all that you desire during this physical lifetime you are experiencing, and each of us is doing all we can to aid and assist you. Know that you are loved. Feel that love deep within you. Realign and reconnect with the love we send to you. Feel it deep in your soul. Be joyful, for you are loved.

You are the star

Y ou are the star. You are the star of your life. You are the central focus of the entire universe. You must have this attitude to have the fullest possible experience in physical. You must be at the top, at the center, in the lead, the star of your life journey. That is why you're here. Even if you choose not to claim this title for yourself, it remains true. So, embrace your stardom, encourage your star power. You are wonderful and amazing. We wish for you to shine.

You are like a gentle flower

You are like a gentle flower. Allow yourself to blossom. You are like a gentle flower, full of color, light, and possibilities. Allow yourself to open gradually. Enjoy the flow of sunlight and fresh breezes. Add your color to the world. This is your time to shine.

You are like the mighty oak tree

You are like the mighty oak tree. Solidly rooted into good earth and soil. You are a provider of energy and life to the planet. You are a taker of energy and life from the plant. All is perfectly balanced. All is perfectly hewn. You are light and love, solid against all weather and storm. Raise your head high toward the blue sky. Feel the strength of the universe through your spine. Feel your roots deep within the earth. This is what it means to be present and in the now. This feeling of connection between you and your planet home.

Be in the middle of things

Be in the middle of things. If you're doing it right, if you're living correctly, you are always right in the middle of things, especially the drama and experience of your own life. Of course, your life doesn't have to be dramatic all the time, but when there's drama, you should be at the center, in the middle, the one in the muck. If you're in someone else's muck, well, it's probably time for you to evaluate your journey.

Create the mood

*C*reate the mood. You create the mood you're in. You decide and determine how you feel. It is all on your shoulders, all your responsibility. No one can ever cause you to feel anything. You create that feeling, that mood. So, begin reaching for the better feelings, the thoughts that will help you to feel better, the experiences that will help you to feel better. You create your mood.

Meditate daily

M editate daily. It has been a while since we have reminded you to meditate each day. This doesn't need to be a marathon session, just five or ten minutes each day of quiet mind meditation, or as close as you can possibly get to quiet mind. Those few minutes, which best serve you early in your day, will set you up for an easier flow of inspiration, ideas, and life in general. So, turn on your favorite woogie music, breathe deeply (we recommend, three beats of breath in, hold for two beats, and then five beats to release that breath), and release all thought. If releasing all thought proves difficult, then, set a single picture in your mind to focus upon, say a lovely flower, a fluffy cloud, a blackboard, etc. Five minutes of focusing on an object in your mind, is very close to quiet mind and in the beginning will get you further toward enlightenment than chastising yourself for not having a quiet mind.

Know that you are loved.

Allow allowing

Allow allowing. You are master creators. You constantly know whether you want more of something you are experiencing or that you want something different. Then, every so often, you simply fall into alignment every once in a while with the new thing or experience you desire. Yet, if you would simply allow yourself to be allowing, if you would simply ask for and expect allowing, the universe could simply and easily bring you the new thing and the new thing and the new thing.... Allow allowing in your life. Know that manifestation is easy if you'll only allow it to be so.

Lighten up

*L*ighten up. Stop taking life so seriously. Stop, just stop. Everything is and can be so much easier if you allow it to be so. Life, your life, this physical life you are now experiencing, is meant to be fun, joyous, interesting, passionate, and enjoyable. Life is simply supposed to be fun. And, it would be more fun for you if you'd only lighten up a little and look for moments to enjoy. Stop creating so much drama and just enjoy your existence.

Look for change

*L*ook for change. All around you, your physical world is always, constantly changing. Be aware of this change. Look for this change. Look to this change to guide you toward your next want and desire. Each subtle change is an indication that perceptions and wants change. Desires change. Lives are constantly changing. Everything is constantly in motion and moving forward toward its next want and desire. For, everything is and has consciousness; therefore, everything has wants and desires and is moving toward and changing into an aligned state with those wants and desires.

Be gentle

Be gentle. Be gentle and easy with yourself. You are, after all, only human. You are not in physical to be or find perfection. You are not in physical to go the easy way at all times. No, you have come to physical to muck it up. You are here to explore, discover, find new ideas, follow new pursuits, make mistakes, take chances, piss people off, be pissed off yourself, find and lose love, find and seek joy and happiness, feel an ever shifting world beneath your feet and ever changing weather and skies above your head. You are here to mix it up and to be. So, be gentle about it all. Take everything in stride. Feel what you feel and be happy and satisfied to be a human being in this space and time. It truly is what you wanted, to be here, right now, feeling this emotion you are now feeling. Be gentle and allowing of your journey. Be gentle.

Yes, find joyful

*Y*es, find joyful. That's your job. That's the task before you. That's the goal: Continually finding joyful. It moves about a lot. It's rarely in the same place. It's rarely caused by the same experiences more than a few times. Being joyful is the reach. Finding joyful from where you are at any given emotional moment. It's a test. A trial. It's life to be in search of joyful. Relish it when you do discover it for it might be fleeting. Or, it might joyfully linger. Enjoy joyful. Seek joyful. Live your life on a journey toward knowing joyful.

Yes, allow

Yes, allow. It is good to allow. Allow each experience to roll past you. Allow each emotion to roll over you. Allow each drop of universal Source Energy to roll through you. This is your journey. It matters not what others think of you. It matters only what you want and desire. Allow others to be on their own journeys. Allow them to take care of themselves and their own emotions, while you, on your journey, experience fully your own emotions and experiences. Allow your life to be your life. Yes, allow.

Yes, movement

Yes, movement. Move with the energy of the universe. Create movement in your life. This might come in physical ways, like swimming, walking, biking, exercising. Or, it might come in spiritual ways like daily meditation, thought, allowing, healing. The best option, when possible, is the combination of the two: physical movement and thought. For, physical movement is an acknowledgement that you are manifested in physical and that you have great respect for your physical body; the latter, thought movement, is your acknowledgement that you are connected to Source Energy, the divine planetary energy and your source for physical life. This is among the greatest and most perfect combinations that we have yet created to spur growth and expansion of All That Is. Enjoy it. Revel in it. Move in, though, and beyond it.

Go with your flow

Go with your flow. It's your flow of energy that we think you should try your best to go with, not the flow of others around you. Don't get involved in the drama and flow of other's energy, unless you enjoy that. Instead, follow your own energy; follow your own path; follow your own desires; follow your own created manifestations. How? How do you find and then follow your own energy flow? Stop everything you've been doing. Quiet your mind for a moment or more. Listen to your inner being. Not the naggy voice you sometimes hear, but the true, inner you. Follow those loving positive thoughts and directions. If the thoughts and directions aren't coming from a loving voice, if they don't sound loving and supportive, that's the naggy voice to ignore. Go with your flow.

It's irrelevant

*I*t's irrelevant. What others think is irrelevant to your emotional being. You determine your emotions and emotional state, not others. That includes what they think, what they say, and what they do. They can't create in your experience, emotional or otherwise. That responsibility falls solidly in your own thoughts. So, release others. Know they can't create for you, only you can do that. Know that you hold every bit of power in your creation process and what you do with that power, what you create, and what you align with is up to you, not another. Others are irrelevant in your creation process.

Just be

*J*ust be. Relax. Breathe. Just be you. There's absolutely no one else to please. There's no one outside of you who expects or requires anything of you. There is nothing to do but follow your most joyful path and direction. Just be. Just be you. Just breathe. Just be.

Everything is your creation

*E*verything is your creation. Everything you encounter and experience is your creation. Everything you experience is you aligning vibrationally with that which you've created. Revel in your power. And, know that if you love something more of it or similar is waiting for you. If you hate something, more of that is also waiting for you unless you alter your vibration to begin aligning with something new and different. Enjoy the contrast and the experience for they are helping you determine what you want more of what you want to be different in your physical experience.

Life is a continuum

*L*ife is a continuum. You are here in physical, you are here in energy form, you are here in both physical and energy form, you are here in energy form. You are always here in energy form, even when your focus is somewhere else. Each of you is an integral part of All That Is, so you are always part of everything. You are here always. Your energy and your creation continue for you are always here.

Allow change

*A*llow change. Nothing was meant to stay the same. Each experience, person, emotion, breath is meant to be different, changing, evolving, becoming something new and different. So, allow change. Feel the emotional restructure and experience of change, but then see new options and potential. See change and allow change and expect change. For, change is what you've requested so you can't expect some things to stay the same while others change. Allow change in all things, most of all, yourself.

This is your life

*T*his is your life. Think for yourself. Make your own choices. Aim to please yourself first and know that if others are pleased by your choices also, well, that's a bonus. Your journey is about you first. Yes, you are co-creating all the time with others, but know that those co-creations are about you first and them second. Your journey, like all physical journeys, is a personal, selfish, muck it up kind of journey. Allow it to be so. Allow yourself to see your own way, make your own choices, speak your own mind, and be your own person along your own, lovely, wonderful journey.

You are never lost

You are never lost. No matter how you feel at any moment, you are always and will always be connected to Source Energy. You are always one with your inner being. You can never be separated or off your path. The area or experiences may seem unfamiliar to you, even unknown, but you are not lost. You are simply on your journey. Turn to your divine guidance system. Ask your inner being or that which you think of as god, for they are the same thing, for aid, guidance, assistance, inspiration, knowledge, etc. You will never be disappointed by the outcome of listening to your true self, your inner being, that which you think of as a god.

Ask for more

A sk for more. You have gotten into the habit of not asking. Or, some of you ask, but not for everything you want, just part of it. You don't want to seem greedy. Or, you have some sense or emotional experience that when you ask it is not given and you are disappointed. We say, ask. Ask. Ask. Ask. And, then know that it is coming and stop asking for what you've already asked for. Yes, ask then for new or different things, but whatever you've already asked for is on its way. The receiving and the asking are at different vibrations, so you've got to let go of the asking and know that the manifestation is in your path. You must be in the new, receiving, answering, manifesting vibration to receive that which you've asked for.

Your path is always lit

Your path is always lit. It's just that sometimes you've closed your eyes or you're looking in a different direction at a shiny object or interesting view. Know, that with very little effort, you can refocus clearly and easily back upon the easiest direction toward that which you have created. Take just a moment to awaken, quiet your mind, and you shall once again easily see and know the well-lit path of your physical journey.

Think well of food

*T*hink well of food. There is nothing you cannot consume that will make you and keep you healthy and well. You only must believe that that which you consume will keep you healthy and well. Everyone seems to have an opinion about health and wellness, and about your health and wellness. But, know that your own personal health and wellness is solely, purely, and absolutely your creation and your manifestation. It is completely based on your own belief systems. Whatever you're currently going through is based on your belief systems. Know that where you're headed is based on your belief systems. And, know absolutely that you can change your beliefs at any moment of your life experience.

Take another step

*T*ake another step. It matters not toward what, simply take another step. And, then take another step. That's how easy the life journey and life path are. That is all you agreed to do when you came here in physical. Take a step and then take another step. Decide what seems interesting and take a step toward that. Decide how that feels and take your next step toward or away from that. Truly, that is your life path. It is that simple. It is that easy, or that difficult. But, that is why you're here. Take a step and then take another step.

You are here

You are here. So, be here. Feel here. Know here. Breathe deeply. Feel fully. Experience everything. Be here, in this moment, in this now. And, now, you are here. So, be here. Feel here. Know here. Breathe deeply. Feel fully. Experience everything. Be here, in this moment, in this now. And, now, you are here. So, be here. Feel here. Know here. Breathe deeply. Feel fully. Experience everything. Be here, in this moment, in this now. And, now, you are here...

Maintain perspective

Maintain perspective. Everything you experience is through your own perspective. Everything you see others experiencing is also through your perspective, not theirs. So, be open and allowing of others to have their experiences. They have created them, you are only viewing them. And, you can't be in their creation process or their manifestations. You can't experience their emotions. So, be. Just be on your own journey and allow others to be on their journey. Feel what you feel about everything, but don't impose your feelings on others. Finally, for the moment, don't feel you know or understand the emotional experiences of another. Everything is an individual's perception, so only they know how they feel.

It's no big deal

*I*t's no big deal. Life is what you make of it. Each moment and situation is always what you make of it. Generally speaking, whatever you have going on at this moment is really no big deal, not in the grand spectrum of the universe and All That Is. And, yet, whatever you have going on at this moment is expanding All That Is, the entire universe. So, it is a huge deal. From the universal perspective, there will be expansion no matter how you choose to deal or not deal with this very moment. It happens whether you are a willing or unwilling participant. We in nonphysical get the full benefit of your experience whether you enjoy your moment or not. So, lighten up. Stop making this moment a big deal. Let go of the drama. Just be. Just be fine with this moment. Enjoy the journey as much as possible and know that the universe will be fine and will continue to expand no matter what you choose or how you choose to experience it.

You know everything

You know everything. You already know all you need to about navigating the human experience. Simply travel your journey, feel fully every emotion, decide if you want more of the same or something different, tell that story, allow yourself to align with the manifestation. It's all "that easy." So, live your life. Be on your journey. Have your own experiences. Stop worrying what others think. Reach always for joy.

About Gregory A. Kompes

L as Vegas Psychic Intuitive Gregory A. Kompes is the scribe for The Three Sisters.

Gregory has written Circuitous Course: A Co-Created Life, Suddenly Psychic: Core Messages to Enhance your Psychic Journey, Message from The Three Sisters, Volumes 1, 2 & 3, the novels Sky Pirates, The Middle Man, Flash Mob, and First Dimension, and the bestselling 50 Fabulous Gay-Friendly Places to Live. He has also penned hundreds of articles on writing, travel, dogs, hiking, and psychic abilities and is included in a dozen anthologies, among them Chicken Soup for the Soul: What I Learned from the Dog.

Gregory offers the online Writer Workshop to help writers improve their craft, leads the Fiction Series for the Gibson Public Library's Creative Writing program (Henderson, NV), and is President of the Henderson Writers' Group (Host of the Las Vegas Writer's Conference) where he leads the group's weekly writer's workshops. Gregory also hosts regular psychic Q&A events that are open to the public.

Gregory holds a BA in English Literature from Columbia University, New York, a B. Msc. in Metaphysics from Sedona University, a Certificate in Online Teaching and Learning, an MS Ed. from California State University, East Bay, and an MFA in Creative Writing from National University.